THE FUTURE OF HUMANITY

THE FUTURE OF HUMANITY

A CONVERSATION

J. Krishnamurti
& David Bohm

1817

Harper & Row, Publishers, San Francisco

Cambridge, Hagerstown, New York, Philadelphia
London, Mexico City, São Paulo, Singapore, Sydney

FIRST EDITION

Library of Congress Cataloging-in-Publication Data

Krishnamurti, J. (Jiddu), 1895–
   The future of humanity.

   "Prepared from dialogues that took place . . . at
Brockwood Park, England, on June 11 and 20, 1983"—P.
   1. Man.   I. Bohm, David.   II. Title.
B5134.K753F87 1986   128   85-45740
ISBN 0-06-064797-3

86 87 88 89 90 HC 10 9 8 7 6 5 4 3 2 1

This book has been prepared from
Dialogues that took place between
J. Krishnamurti and Professor David Bohm
at Brockwood Park, England,
on June 11 and 20, 1983.

CONTENTS

PREFACE

The two dialogues which appear in this book took place three years after a series of thirteen similar dialogues between Krishnamurti and myself, which appeared in the book "The Ending of Time."* Therefore they were inevitably profoundly affected by what had been done in these earlier dialogues. In a certain sense, therefore, the two books deal with closely related questions. Of course, "The Ending of Time" can, because of its much greater length, go into these questions in a more thorough and extensive way. Nevertheless, the present book stands by itself; it approaches the problems of human life in its own way, and provides important additional insights into these problems. Moreover, I feel that it is an easier book to follow, and may therefore usefully serve as an introduction to "The Ending of Time."

The starting point for our discussions was the question: "What is the future of humanity?" This question is by now of vital concern to everyone, because modern science and technology are clearly seen to have opened up immense possibilities of destruction. It soon became clear as we talked together that the ultimate origin of this

*Harper & Row, 1985.

situation is in the generally confused mentality of mankind, which has not changed basically in this respect throughout the whole of recorded history and probably for much longer than this. Evidently, it was essential to inquire deeply into the root of this difficulty if there is ever to be a possibility that humanity will be diverted from its present very dangerous course.

These dialogues constitute a serious inquiry into this problem, and as they proceeded, many of the basic points of Krishnamurti's teachings emerged. Thus, the question of the future of humanity seems, at first sight, to imply that a solution must involve time in a fundamental way. Yet, as Krishnamurti points out, psychological time, or "becoming," is the very source of the destructive current that is putting the future of humanity at risk. To question time in this way, however, is to question the adequacy of knowledge and thought, as a means of dealing with this problem. But if knowledge and thought are not adequate, what is it that is actually required? This led in turn to the question of whether mind is limited by the brain of mankind, with all the knowledge that it has accumulated over the ages. This knowledge, which now conditions us deeply, has produced what is, in effect, an irrational and self-destructive program in which the brain seems to be helplessly caught up.

If mind is limited by such a state of the brain, then the future of humanity must be very grim indeed. Krishnamurti does not, however, regard these limitations as inevitable. Rather, he emphasizes that mind is essentially free of the distorting bias that is inherent in the conditioning of the brain, and that through insight arising in proper undirected attention without a center, it can change the cells of the brain and remove the destructive conditioning. If this is so, then it is crucially important that there be this kind of attention, and that we give to this question the same intensity of energy that we generally give to other activities of life that are really of vital interest to us.

At this point, it is worth remarking that modern research into the brain and nervous system actually gives considerable support to Krishnamurti's statement that insight may change the brain cells. Thus, for example, it is now well known that there are important substances in the body, the hormones and the neurotransmitters, that fundamentally affect the entire functioning of the brain and nervous system. These substances respond, from moment to moment, to what a person knows, to what he thinks, and to what all this means to him. It is by now fairly well established that in this way the brain cells and their functioning are profoundly affected by knowledge and thought, especially when these give rise to strong feelings and passions. It is thus quite plausible that insight, which must arise in a state of great mental energy and passion, could change the brain cells in an even more profound way.

What has been said here necessarily gives only a brief outline of what is in the dialogues, and cannot show the full scope and depth of the inquiry that takes place within them into the nature of human consciousness and of the problems that have arisen in this consciousness. Indeed, I would say that the result has been a concise and easily readable book, which contains the essential spirit of the whole of Krishnamurti's teachings, and throws an important further light on them.

David Bohm

ONE

DAVID BOHM: There are several problems that we might discuss. One is, when a person is just starting out he has to make a living. There are very few opportunities now, and most of these are in jobs which are extremely limited.

J. KRISHNAMURTI: And there is unemployment throughout the world. I wonder what he would do, knowing that the future is grim, very depressing, dangerous, and so uncertain. Where would you begin?

DB: Well I think one would have to stand back from all the particular problems of one's own needs and the needs of people around one.

JK: Are you saying one should really forget oneself for the time being?

DB: Yes.

JK: Even if I did forget myself, when I look at this world in which I am going to live, and have some kind of career or profession, what would I do? This is a problem that I think most young people are facing.

DB: Yes. That's clear. Well, have you something that you would suggest?

JK: You see I don't think in terms of evolution.

DB: I understand that. That's the point I was expecting we would discuss.

JK: I don't think there is psychological evolution at all.

DB: We have discussed this quite often so I think I understand to some extent what you mean. But I think that people who are new to this are not going to understand.

JK: Yes, we will discuss this whole question, if you will. Why are we concerned about the future? Surely the whole future is now.

DB: In a sense the whole future is now, but we have to make that clear. It goes very much against the whole way of thinking, of the tradition of mankind. . . .

JK: I know. Mankind thinks in terms of evolution, continuance, and so on.

DB: Perhaps we could approach it in another way? That is, evolution seems in the present era to be the most natural way to think. So I would like to ask you what objections you have to thinking in terms of evolution. Could I explain a point? This word evolution has many meanings.

JK: Of course. We are talking psychologically.

DB: Now the first point is, let's dispose of it physically.

JK: An acorn will grow into an oak.

DB: Also the species have evolved: for example, from the plants to the animals and to man.

JK: Yes, we have taken a million years to be what we are.

DB: You have no question that that has happened?

JK: No, that has happened.

DB: It may continue to happen.

JK: That is evolution.

DB: That is a valid process.

JK: Of course.

DB: It takes place in time. And, therefore, in that region the past, present, and future are important.

JK: Yes obviously. I don't know a certain language, I need time to learn it.

DB: Also it takes time to improve the brain. You see, if the brain started out small, and then it got bigger and bigger, that took a million years.

JK: And it becomes much more complex, and so on. All that needs time. All that is movement in space and time.

DB: Yes. So you will admit physical time and neuro-physiological time.

JK: Neuro-physiological time, absolutely. Of course. Any sane man would.

7

DB: Now most people also admit psychological time, what they call mental time.

JK: Yes, that is what we are talking about. Whether there is such a thing as psychological tomorrow, psychological evolution.

DB: Or yesterday. Now at first sight I am afraid this will sound strange. It seems I can remember yesterday. And there is tomorrow; I can anticipate. And it has happened many times, you know days have succeeded each other. So I do have the experience of time, from yesterday to today to tomorrow.

JK: Of course. That is simple enough.

DB: Now what is it that you are denying?

JK: I deny that I will be something, become better.

DB: I can change . . . but now there are two ways of looking at that. One approach is, will I intentionally become better because I am trying? Or is evolution a natural, inevitable process, in which we are being swept along as if in a current, and perhaps becoming better, or worse, or finding that something is happening to us.

JK: Psychologically.

DB: Psychologically, which takes time, which may not be the result of my trying to become better. It may or may not be. Some people think one way, some another. But are you denying also that there is a kind of natural psychological evolution as there was a natural biological evolution?

8

JK: I am denying that, yes.

DB: Now why do you deny it?

JK: Because, first of all, what is the psyche, the me, the ego, and so on? What is it?

DB: The word psyche has many meanings. It may mean the mind, for example. Do you mean that the ego is the same thing?

JK: The ego. I am talking of the ego, the me.

DB: Yes. Now some people think there will be an evolution in which the me is transcended, that it will rise to a higher level.

JK: Yes, will the transition need time?

DB: A transcendence, a transition.

JK: Yes. That is my whole question.

DB: So there are two questions: one is, will the me ever improve? And the other is, even if we suppose we want to get beyond the me, can that be done in time?

JK: That cannot be done in time.

DB: Now we have to make it clear why not.

JK: Yes. I will. We will go into it. What is the me? If the psyche has such different meanings, the me is the whole movement which thought has brought about.

DB: Why do you say that?

JK: The me is the consciousness, my consciousness: the me is my name, form, and all the experiences, remembrances, and so on that I have had. The whole structure of the me is put together by thought.

DB: That again would be something which some people might find it hard to accept.

JK: Of course. We are discussing it.

DB: Now the first experience, the first feeling I have about the me is that it is there independently and that the me is thinking.

JK: Is the me independent of my thinking?

DB: Well my own first feeling is that the me is there independent of my thinking. And that it is the me that is thinking, you see.

JK: Yes.

DB: Just as I am here, and I could move; I could move my arm, I could think, or I could move my head. Now is that an illusion?

JK: No.

DB: Why?

JK: Because when I move my arm there is the intention to grasp something, to take something, which is first the movement of thought. That makes the arm move, and so on. My contention is—and I am ready to accept it as false or true—that thought is the basis of all this.

10

DB: Yes. Your contention is that the whole sense of the me and what it is doing is coming out of thought. Now what you mean by thought is not merely intellectual?

JK: No, of course not. Thought is the movement of experience, knowledge, and memory. It is this whole movement.

DB: It sounds to me as if you mean the consciousness as a whole.

JK: As a whole, that's right.

DB: And you are saying that that movement is the me?

JK: The whole content of that consciousness is the me. That me is not different from my consciousness.

DB: Yes. I think one could say that I am my consciousness, for if I am not conscious I am not here.

JK: Of course.

DB: Now is consciousness nothing but what you have just described, which includes thought, feeling, intention? . . .

JK: . . . intention, aspirations . . .

DB: . . . memories . . .

JK: . . . memories, beliefs, dogmas, the rituals that are performed. The whole, like the computer that has been programmed.

DB: Yes. Now that certainly is in consciousness. Everybody would agree, but many people would feel that there is more to it than that; that consciousness may go beyond that.

JK: Let's go into it. The content of our consciousness makes up the consciousness.

DB: Yes, I think that requires some understanding. The ordinary use of the word content is quite different. If you say that the content of a glass is water, the glass is one thing and the water is another.

JK: Consciousness is made up of all that it has remembered: beliefs, dogmas, rituals, fears, pleasures, sorrow.

DB: Yes. Now if all that were absent, would there be no consciousness?

JK: Not as we know it.

DB: But there would still be a kind of consciousness?

JK: A totally different kind. But consciousness, as we know it, is all that.

DB: As we generally know it.

JK: Yes. And that is the result of multiple activities of thought. Thought has put all this together, which is my consciousness—the reactions, the responses, the memories—extraordinary, complex intricacies and subtleties. All that makes up consciousness.

DB: As we know it.

JK: But does that consciousness have a future?

DB: Yes. Does it have a past?

JK: Of course. Remembrance.

DB: Remembrance, yes. Why do you say it has no future then?

JK: If it has a future it will be exactly the same kind of thing, moving. The same activities, the same thoughts, modified, but the pattern will be repeated over and over again.

DB: Are you saying that thought can only repeat?

JK: Yes.

DB: But there is a feeling, for example, that thought can develop new ideas.

JK: But thought is limited because knowledge is limited.

DB: Well, yes, that might require some discussion.

JK: Yes, we must discuss it.

DB: Why do you say knowledge is always limited?

JK: Because you, as a scientist, are experimenting, adding, searching. And after you some other person will add more. So knowledge, which is born of experience, is limited.

DB: But some people have said it isn't. They would hope to obtain perfect, or absolute, knowledge of the laws of nature.

JK: The laws of nature are not the laws of human beings.

DB: Well, do you want to restrict the discussion then to knowledge about the human being?

JK: Of course, that's all we can talk about.

DB: Even there, it is a question of whether that knowledge of nature is possible too.

JK: Yes. We are talking about the future of humanity.

DB: So are we saying that man cannot obtain unlimited knowledge of the psyche?

JK: That's right.

DB: There is always more that is unknown.

JK: Yes. There is always more and more unknown. So if once we admit that knowledge is limited, then thought is limited.

DB: Yes, thought depends on knowledge, and the knowledge does not cover everything. Therefore thought will not be able to handle everything that happens.

JK: That's right. But that is what the politicians and all the other people are doing. They think thought can solve every problem.

DB: Yes. You can see in the case of politicians that knowledge is very limited, in fact it is almost nonexistent!

And, therefore, when you lack adequate knowledge of what you are dealing with, you create confusion.

JK: Yes. So then as thought is limited, our consciousness, which has been put together by thought, is limited.

DB: Now can you make that clear? That means we can only stay in the same circle.

JK: The same circle.

DB: You see, one of the ideas might be, if you compare with science, that people might think although their knowledge is limited they are constantly discovering.

JK: What you discover is added to, but is still limited.

DB: It is still limited. That's the point. I can keep on; I think one of the ideas behind a scientific approach is that, though knowledge is limited, I can discover and keep up with the actuality.

JK: But that is also limited.

DB: My discoveries are limited. And there is always the unknown which I have not discovered.

JK: That is what I am saying. The unknown, the limitless, cannot be captured by thought.

DB: Yes.

JK: Because thought in itself is limited. You and I agree to that; we not only agree but it is a fact.

DB: Perhaps we could bring it out still more. That is, thought is limited, even though we might intellectually consider that thought is not limited. There is a very strong predisposition, tendency, to feel that way—that thought can do anything.

JK: Anything. It can't. See what it has done in the world.

DB: Well, I agree that it has done some terrible things, but that doesn't prove that it is always wrong. You see, perhaps you could blame it on the people who have used it wrongly.

JK: I know, that is a good old trick! But thought in itself is limited, therefore whatever it does is limited.

DB: Yes, and you are saying that it is limited in a very serious way.

JK: That's right. Of course in a very, very serious way.

DB: Could we bring that out? Say what that way is?

JK: That way is what is happening in the world.

DB: All right, let's look at that.

JK: The totalitarian ideals are the invention of thought.

DB: The very word totalitarian means that people wanted to cover the totality, but they couldn't.

JK: They couldn't.

DB: The thing collapsed.

JK: It is collapsing.

DB: But then there are those who say they are not totalitarians.

JK: But the democrats, the republicans, the idealists, and so on, all their thinking is limited.

DB: Yes, and it is limited in a way that is . . .

JK: . . . very destructive.

DB: Now, could we bring that out? You see I could say, "All right my thought is limited, but it may not be all that serious." Why is this so important?

JK: That is fairly simple: because whatever action is born of limited thought must inevitably breed conflict.

DB: Yes.

JK: Like dividing humanity religiously, or into nationalities, and so on, has created havoc in the world.

DB: Yes, now let's connect that with the limitation of thought. My knowledge is limited: how does that lead me to divide the world into . . .

JK: Aren't we seeking security?

DB: Yes.

JK: And we thought there was security in the family, in the tribe, in nationalism. So we thought there was security in division.

DB: Yes. Now it has come out. Take the tribe, for example: one may feel insecure, and one then says "With the tribe I am secure." That is a conclusion. And I think

I know enough to be sure that is so—but I don't. Other things happen that I don't know, which make that very insecure. Other tribes come along.

JK: No, no! The very division creates insecurity.

DB: Yes, it helps to create it, but I am trying to say that I don't know enough to know that. I don't *see* that.

JK: But one doesn't see it because one has not thought about anything, not looked at the world, as a whole.

DB: Well the thought which aims at security attempts to know everything important. As soon as it knows everything important it says "This will bring security." But there are a lot of things it still doesn't know, and one is that this very thought itself is divisive.

JK: Yes. In itself it is limited. Anything that is limited must inevitably create conflict. If I say I am an individual, that is limited.

DB: Yes.

JK: I am concerned with myself, that is very limited.

DB: We have to make this clear. If I say this is a table which is limited, it creates no conflict.

JK: No, there is no conflict there.

DB: But when I say, this is "me," that creates conflict.

JK: The "me" is a divisive entity.

DB: Let us see more clearly why.

JK: Because it is separate; it is concerned with itself. The "me" identifying with the greater nation is still divisive.

DB: I define myself in the interest of security so that I know what I am as opposed to what you are, and I protect myself. Now this creates a division between me and you.

JK: We and they, and so on.

DB: Now that comes from my limited thought, because I don't understand that we are really closely related and connected.

JK: We are human beings, and all human beings have more or less the same problems.

DB: No, I haven't understood that. My knowledge is limited; I think that we can make a distinction and protect ourselves, and me, and not the others.

JK: Yes, that's right.

DB: But in the very act of doing that I create instability.

JK: That's right, insecurity. So if not merely intellectually or verbally but actually, we feel that we are the rest of humanity, then the responsibility becomes immense.

DB: Well, how can you do anything about that responsibility?

JK: Then I either contribute to the whole mess, or keep out of it.

DB: I think we have touched upon an important point. We say the whole of humanity, of mankind, is one, and therefore to create division is . . .

JK: . . . dangerous.

DB: Yes. Whereas to create division between me and the table is not dangerous, because in some sense we are not one.

JK: Of course.

DB: That is, only in some very general sense are we at one. Now mankind doesn't realize that it is all one.

JK: Why?

DB: Let's go into it. This is a crucial point. There are so many divisions, not only between nations and religions but between one person and another.

JK: Why is there this division?

DB: The feeling is, at least in the modern era, that every human being is an individual. This may not have been so strong in the past.

JK: That is what I question. I question altogether whether we are individuals.

DB: That is a big question. . . .

JK: Of course. We said just now that the consciousness which is me is similar to the rest of mankind. They all suffer, all have fears, are insecure; they have their own particular gods and rituals, all put together by thought.

DB: I think there are two questions here. One is, not everybody feels that he is similar to others. Most people feel they have some unique distinction. . . .

JK: What do you mean by "unique distinction"? Distinction in doing something?

DB: There may be many things. For example, one nation may feel that it is able to do certain things better than another; one person has some special things he does, or a particular quality. . . .

JK: Of course. Somebody else is better in this or that.

DB: He may take pride in his own special abilities, or advantages.

JK: But when you put away that, basically we are the same.

DB: You are saying these things which you have just described are . . .

JK: . . . superficial.

DB: Yes. Now what are the things that are basic?

JK: Fear, sorrow, pain, anxiety, loneliness, and all the human travail.

DB: But many people might feel that the basic things are the highest achievements of man. For one thing, people may feel proud of man's achievement in science and art and culture and technology.

JK: We have achieved in all those directions, certainly. In technology, communication, travel, medicine, surgery, we have advanced tremendously.

DB: Yes, it is really remarkable in many ways.

JK: There is no question about it. But what have we psychologically achieved?

DB: None of this has affected us psychologically.

JK: Yes, that's right.

DB: And the psychological question is more important than any of the others, because if the psychological question is not cleared up the rest is dangerous.

JK: Yes. If we are psychologically limited, then whatever we do will be limited, and the technology will then be used by our limited . . .

DB: . . . yes, the master is this limited psyche, and not the rational structure of technology. And in fact technology then becomes a dangerous instrument. So that is one point, that the psyche is at the core of it all, and if the psyche is not in order then the rest is useless. Then, although we are saying there are certain basic disorders in the psyche common to us all, we may all have a potential for something else. The next point is are we all one really? Even though we are all similar, that doesn't mean we are all the same, that we are all one.

JK: We said, in our consciousness basically we all have the same ground on which we stand.

DB: Yes, from the fact that the human body is similar, but that doesn't prove they are all the same.

JK: Of course not. Your body is different from mine.

DB: Yes, we are in different places, we are different entities, and so on. But I think you are saying that the consciousness is not an entity which is individual. . . .

JK: That's right.

DB: The body is an entity which has a certain individuality.

JK: That all seems so clear. Your body is different from mine. I have a different name from you.

DB: Yes, we are different. Though of similar material we are different. We can't exchange because the proteins in one body may not agree with those in the other. Now many people feel that way about the mind, saying that there is a chemistry between people which may agree or disagree.

JK: Yes but actually if you go deeper into the question, consciousness is shared by all human beings.

DB: Now the feeling is that the consciousness is individual and that it is communicated. . . .

JK: I think that is an illusion, because we are sticking to something that is not true.

23

DB: Do you want to say that there is one consciousness of mankind?

JK: It is all one.

DB: That is important, because whether it is many or
one is a crucial question.

JK: Yes.

DB: It could be many, which are then communicating
and building up the larger unit. Or are you saying that
from the very beginning it is all one?

JK: From the very beginning it is all one.

DB: And the sense of separateness is an illusion?

JK: That is what I am saying, over and over again.
That seems so logical, sane. The other is insanity.

DB: Yes, but people don't feel, at least not immediately, that the notion of separate existence is insane,
because one extrapolates from the body to the mind.
One says, it is quite sensible to say my body is separate
from yours, and inside my body is my mind. Now are you
saying that the mind is not inside the body?

JK: That is quite a different question. Let's finish with
the other first. *Each one of us* thinks that we *are separate
individuals,* psychically. . . . What we have done in the
world is a colossal mess.

DB: Well if we think we are separate when we are not
separate, then it will clearly be a colossal mess.

JK: That is what is happening. Each one thinks he has to do what he wants to do; fulfill himself. So he is struggling in his separateness to achieve peace, to achieve security, and that security and peace are totally denied.

DB: The reason they are denied is because there is no separation. You see, if there were really separation it would be a rational thing to try to do. But if we are trying to separate what is inseparable the result will be chaos.

JK: That's right.

DB: Now that is clear, but I think that it will not be clear to people immediately that the consciousness of mankind is one inseparable whole.

JK: Yes, an inseparable whole.

DB: Many questions will arise if we consider the notion, but I don't know if we have gone far enough into this yet. One question is, why do we think we are separate?

JK: Why do I think I am separate? That is my conditioning.

DB: Yes, but how did we ever adopt such a foolish conditioning?

JK: From childhood, it is mine, my toy, not yours.

DB: But the first feeling I get of "it is mine" is because I feel I am separate. It isn't clear how the mind, which was one, came to this illusion that it is all broken up into many pieces.

JK: I think it is again the activity of thought. Thought in its very nature is divisive, fragmentary, and therefore I am a fragment.

DB: Thought will create a sense of fragments. You could see, for example, that once we decide to set up a nation we will think we are separate from other nations, and all sorts of consequences follow which make the whole thing seem independently real. We have separate language, a separate flag, and we set up a boundary. And after a while we see so much evidence of separation that we forget how it started, and say it was there always, and that we are merely proceeding from what was there always.

JK: Of course. That's why I feel that if once we grasp the nature and structure of thought, how thought operates, what is the source of thought—and therefore it is always limited—if we really see that, then . . .

DB: Now the source of thought is what? Is it memory?

JK: Memory. The remembrance of things past, which is knowledge, and knowledge is the outcome of experience, and experience is always limited.

DB: Thought also includes, of course, the attempt to go forward, to use logic, to take into account discoveries and insights.

JK: As we were saying some time ago, thought is time.

DB: All right. Thought is time. That requires more discussion too, because the first response is to say time is there first, and thought is taking place in time.

JK: Ah, no.

DB: For example, if movement is taking place, if the body is moving, this requires time.

JK: To go from here to there needs time. To learn a language needs time.

DB: Yes. To grow a plant needs time.

JK: To paint a picture takes time.

DB: We also say that to think takes time.

JK: So we think in terms of time.

DB: Yes, the first point that one would tend to look at is whether just as everything takes time, to think takes time? Are you saying something else, which is that thought is time?

JK: Thought is time.

DB: That is psychologically speaking.

JK: Psychologically, of course.

DB: Now how do we understand that?

JK: How do we understand what?

DB: Thought is time. You see it is not obvious.

JK: Oh yes. Would you say thought is movement, and time is movement?

DB: That's movement. You see, time is a mysterious thing: people have argued about it. We could say that time requires movement. I could understand that we cannot have time without movement.

JK: Time is movement. Time is not separate from movement.

DB: I don't say it is separate from movement. . . . You see, if we said time and movement are one . . .

JK: Yes, we are saying that.

DB: They cannot be separated?

JK: No.

DB: That seems fairly clear. Now there is physical movement, which means physical time.

JK: Physical time, hot and cold, and also dark and light . . .

DB: . . . the seasons . . .

JK: . . . sunset and sunrise. All that.

DB: Yes. Now then we have the movement of thought. That brings in the question of the nature of thought. Is thought nothing but a movement in the nervous system, in the brain? Would you say that?

JK: Yes.

DB: Some people have said it includes the movement of the nervous system, but there might be something beyond.

28

JK: What is time, actually? Time is hope.

DB: Psychologically.

JK: Psychologically. I am talking entirely psychologically for the moment. Hope is time. Becoming is time. Achieving is time. Now take the question of becoming: I want to become something, psychologically. I want to become nonviolent. Take that, for example. That is altogether a fallacy.

DB: We understand it is a fallacy, but the reason it is a fallacy is that there is no time of that kind, is that it?

JK: No. Human beings are violent.

DB: Yes.

JK: And they have been talking a great deal—Tolstoy, and in India—of nonviolence. The fact is we are violent. And the nonviolence is not real. But we want to become that.

DB: But it is again an extension of the kind of thought that we have with regard to material things. If you see a desert, the desert is real and you say the garden is not real, but in your mind is the garden which will come when you put the water there. So we say we can plan for the future when the desert will become fertile. Now we have to be careful, we say we are violent but we cannot by similar planning become nonviolent.

JK: No.

DB: Why is that?

JK: Why? Because the nonviolent state cannot exist when there is violence. That's just an ideal.

DB: One has to make this more clear, in the same sense the fertile state and the desert don't exist together either. I think you are saying that in the case of the mind, when you are violent, nonviolence has no meaning.

JK: Violence is the only state.

DB: That is all there is.

JK: Yes, not the other.

DB: The movement towards the other is illusory.

JK: So all ideals are illusory, psychologically. The ideal of building a marvelous bridge is not illusory. You can plan it, but to have psychological ideals . . .

DB: Yes, if you are violent and you continue to be violent while you are trying to be nonviolent, it has no meaning.

JK: No meaning, and yet that has become such an important thing. The becoming, which is either becoming "what is" or becoming away from "what is."

DB: Yes. "What should be." If you say there can be no sense to becoming in the way of self-improvement, that's . . .

JK: Oh, self-improvement is something so utterly ugly. We are saying that the source of all this is a movement of thought as time. When once we have made time, psychologically, all the other ideals, nonviolence, achieving some super state, and so on, become utterly illusory.

DB: Yes. When you talk of the movement of thought as time, it seems to me that that time which comes from the movement of thought is illusory.

JK: Yes.

DB: We sense it as time, but it is not a real kind of time.

JK: That is why we asked, what is time?

DB: Yes.

JK: I need time to go from here to there. I need time if I want to learn engineering. I must study it; it takes time. That same movement is carried over into the psyche. We say, I need time to be good. I need time to be enlightened.

DB: Yes, that will always create a conflict. One part of you and another. So that movement in which you say, I need time, also creates a division in the psyche. Between the observer and the observed.

JK: Yes, we are saying the observer is the observed.

DB: And therefore there is no time, psychologically.

JK: That's right. The experiencer, the thinker, is the thought. There is no thinker separate from thought.

DB: All that you are saying seems very reasonable, but I think that it goes so strongly against the tradition we are

31

used to that it will be extraordinarily hard for people, generally speaking, really to understand.

JK: Most people just want a comfortable way of living: "Let me carry on as I am, for God's sake, leave me alone!"

DB: But that is the result of so much conflict, that people are warned off by it, I think.

JK: But conflict exists, whether we like it or not. So, that is the whole point, is it possible to live a life without conflict?

DB: Yes, that is all implicit in what has been said. The source of conflict is thought, or knowledge, or the past.

JK: So then one asks: is it possible to transcend thought?

DB: Yes.

JK: Or is it possible to end knowledge? I am putting it psychologically. . . .

DB: Yes. We say that knowledge of material objects and things like that, knowledge of science, will continue.

JK: Absolutely. That must continue.

DB: But what you call self-knowledge is what you are asking to end, isn't it?

JK: Yes.

DB: On the other hand people have said—even you have said—that self-knowledge is very important.

JK: Self-knowledge is important, but if I take time to understand myself, I will understand myself eventually by examination, analysis, by watching my whole relationship with others and so on—all that involves time. And I say there is another way of looking at the whole thing without time. Which is, when the observer is the observed.

DB: Yes.

JK: In that observation there is no time.

DB: Could we go into that further? I mean, for example, if you say there is no time, but still you feel that you can remember an hour ago you were someone else. Now in what sense can we say that there is no time?

JK: Time is division. As thought is division. That is why thought is time.

DB: Time is a series of divisions of past, present, future.

JK: Thought is divisive. So time is thought. Or thought is time.

DB: It doesn't exactly follow from what you said. . . .

JK: Let's go into it.

DB: Yes. You see, at first sight one would think that thought makes divisions of all kinds, with the ruler and with all kinds of things, and also divides up intervals of time: past, present and future. Now it doesn't follow, from just that, that thought is time.

33

JK: Look, we said time is movement.

DB: Yes.

JK: Thought is also a series of movements. So both are movements.

DB: Thought is a movement, we suppose, of the nervous system and . . .

JK: You see, it is a movement of becoming. I am talking psychologically.

DB: Psychologically. But, whenever you think, something is also moving in the blood, in the nerves, and so on. Now when you talk of a psychological movement, do you mean just a change of content?

JK: Change of content?

DB: Well what is the movement? What is moving?

JK: Look, I am this, and I am attempting to become something else psychologically.

DB: So that movement is in the content of your thought?

JK: Yes.

DB: If you say "I am this and I am attempting to become that," then I am in movement. At least, I feel I am in movement.

JK: Say, for instance, that I am greedy. Greed is a movement.

DB: What kind of a movement is it?

JK: To get what I want, to get more. It is a movement.

DB: All right.

JK: And I find that movement painful. Then I try not to be greedy.

DB: Yes.

JK: The attempt not to be greedy is a movement of time, is becoming.

DB: Yes, but even the greed was becoming.

JK: Of course. So, is the real question, is it possible not to become, psychologically?

DB: It seems that would require that you should not be anything psychologically. As soon as you define yourself in any way, then . . .

JK: No, we will define it in a minute or two.

DB: I meant, if I define myself as greedy, say that I am greedy, or I am this, or I am that, then either I will want to become something else or to remain what I am.

JK: Now can I remain what I am? Can I remain not with non-greed but with greed? Greed is not different from me; greed is me.

DB: The ordinary way of thinking is that I am here, and I could either be greedy or not greedy.

JK: Of course.

DB: As these are attributes which I may or may not have.

35

JK: But the attributes are me.

DB: Now that again goes very much against our common language and experience.

JK: All the qualities, the attributes, the virtues, the judgments, the conclusions, and opinions are me.

DB: It seems to me that this would have to be perceived immediately. . . .

JK: That is the whole question. To perceive the totality of this whole movement, instantly. Then we come to the point—it sounds a little odd, and perhaps a little crazy, but it is not—is it possible to perceive without all the movement of memory? To perceive something directly without the word, without the reaction, without the memories entering into perception.

DB: That is a very big question, because memory has constantly entered perception. It would raise the question of what is going to stop memory from entering perception?

JK: Nothing can stop it. But if we see the reason, the rationality of the activity of memory which is limited—in the very perception that it is limited, we have moved out of it into another dimension.

DB: It seems to me that you have to perceive the whole of the limitation of memory.

JK: Yes, not one part.

DB: You can see in general that memory is limited, but there are many ways in which this is not obvious. For example, many of our reactions that are not obvious may be memory, but we don't experience them as memory. Suppose I am becoming: I experience greed, and I have the urge to become less greedy. I can remember that I am greedy but think that this "me" is the one who remembers, not the other way around, not that memory creates "me"—right?

JK: All this really comes down to whether humanity can live without conflict. It basically comes to that. Can we have peace on this earth? The activities of thought never bring it about.

DB: It seems clear from what has been said that the activity of thought cannot bring about peace: it inherently brings about conflict.

JK: Yes, if we once really see that, our whole activity would be totally different.

DB: But are you saying then that there is an activity which is not thought? Which is beyond thought?

JK: Yes.

DB: And which is not only beyond thought but which does not require the cooperation of thought? That it is possible for this to go on when thought is absent?

JK: That is the real point. We have often discussed this, whether there is anything beyond thought. Not something holy, sacred—we are not talking of that. We are asking, is there an activity which is not touched by thought? We are saying there is. And that that activity is the highest form of intelligence.

37

DB: Yes, now we have brought in intelligence.

JK: I know, I purposively brought it in! So intelligence is not the activity of cunning thought. There is intelligence to build a cable. . . .

DB: Well, intelligence can use thought, as you have often said. That is, thought can be the action of intelligence—would you put it that way?

JK: Yes.

DB: Or it could be the action of memory?

JK: That's it. Either it is the action born of memory and memory being limited, therefore thought is limited, and it has its own activity which then brings about conflict. . . .

DB: I think this would connect with what people are saying about computers. Every computer must eventually depend on some kind of memory which is put in, programmed. And that must be limited.

JK: Of course.

DB: Therefore when we operate from memory we are not very different from a computer; the other way around perhaps, the computer is not very different from us.

JK: I would say a Hindu has been programmed for the last five thousand years to be a Hindu; or, in this country, you have been programmed as British, or as a Catholic or a Protestant. So we are all programmed to a certain extent.

DB: Yes, but you are bringing in the notion of an intelligence which is free of the program, which is creative, perhaps. . . .

JK: Yes. That intelligence has nothing to do with memory and knowledge.

DB: It may act in memory and knowledge but it is has nothing to do with it. . . .

JK: That's right. I mean, how do you find out whether it has any reality and is not just imagination and romantic nonsense? To come to that, one has to go into the whole question of suffering, whether there is an end to suffering. And as long as suffering and fear and the pursuit of pleasure exist there cannot be love.

DB: There are many questions there. Suffering, pleasure, fear, anger, violence, and greed—all of those are the response of memory.

JK: Yes.

DB: They are nothing to do with intelligence.

JK: They are all part of thought and memory.

DB: And as long as they are going on it seems that intelligence cannot operate in thought, or through thought.

JK: That's right. So there must be freedom from suffering.

DB: Well that is a very key point.

JK: That is really a very serious and deep question. Whether it is possible to end suffering, which is the ending of me.

DB: Yes, it may seem repetitious but the feeling is that I am there, and I either suffer or don't suffer. I either enjoy things or suffer. Now I think you are saying that suffering arises from thought; it is thought.

JK: Identification. Attachment.

DB: So what is it that suffers? Memory may produce pleasure and then when it doesn't work it produces the opposite of the feeling of pleasure—pain and suffering.

JK: Not only that. Suffering is much more complex, isn't it?

DB: Yes.

JK: What is suffering? The meaning of the word is to have pain, to have grief, to feel utterly lost, lonely.

DB: It seems to me that it is not only pain, but a kind of total, very pervasive pain. . . .

JK: But suffering is the loss of someone.

DB: Or the loss of something very important.

JK: Yes, of course. Loss of my wife, my son, brother, or whatever it is, and the desperate sense of loneliness.

DB: Or else just simply the fact that the whole world is going into such a state.

JK: Of course. . . . All the wars.

DB: It makes everything meaningless, you see.

JK: What a lot of suffering wars have created. And wars have been going on for thousands of years. That is why I am saying we are carrying on with the same pattern of the last five thousand years or more. . . .

DB: One can easily see that the violence and hatred in wars will interfere with intelligence.

JK: Obviously.

DB: But some people have felt that by going through suffering they become . . .

JK: . . . intelligent?

DB: . . . Purified, like going through the crucible.

JK: I know. That through suffering you learn. That through suffering your ego is vanished, dissolved.

DB: Yes, dissolved, refined.

JK: It is not. People have suffered immensely, how many wars, how many tears, and the destructive nature of governments? And unemployment, ignorance . . .

DB: . . . ignorance of disease, pain, everything. But what is suffering really? Why does it destroy intelligence, or prevent it? What is going on?

JK: Suffering is a shock; I suffer, I have pain, it is the essence of the "me."

DB: The difficulty with suffering is that it is the me that is there that is suffering.

JK: Yes.

DB: And this me is really being sorry for itself in some way.

JK: My suffering is different from your suffering.

DB: Yes, it isolates itself. It creates an illusion of some kind.

JK: We don't see that suffering is shared by all humanity.

DB: Yes, but suppose we do see it is shared by all humanity?

JK: Then I begin to question what suffering is. It is not my suffering.

DB: That is important. In order to understand the nature of suffering I have to get out of this idea that it is *my* suffering because as long as I believe it is my suffering I have an illusory notion of the whole thing.

JK: And I can never end it.

DB: If you are dealing with an illusion you can do nothing with it. You see why—we have to come back. Why is suffering the suffering of many? At first it seems that I feel pain in the tooth, or else I have a loss, or something has happened to me, and the other person seems perfectly happy.

42

JK: Happy, yes. But also he is suffering in his own way.

DB: Yes. At the moment he doesn't see it, but he has his problems too.

JK: Suffering is common to all humanity.

DB: But the fact that it is common is not enough to make it all one.

JK: It is actual.

DB: Are you saying that the suffering of mankind is all one, inseparable?

JK: Yes, that is what I have been saying.

DB: As is the consciousness of man?

JK: Yes, that's right.

DB: That when anybody suffers, the whole of mankind is suffering.

JK: The whole point is, we have suffered from the beginning of time, and we haven't solved it. We haven't ended suffering.

DB: But I think you have said that the reason we haven't solved it is because we are treating it as personal, or as in a small group . . . and that is an illusion.

JK: Yes.

DB: Now any attempt to deal with an illusion cannot solve anything.

JK: Thought cannot solve anything psychologically.

DB: Because you can say that thought itself divides. Thought is limited and is unable to see that this suffering is all one. And in that way divides it up as mine and yours.

JK: That's right.

DB: And that creates illusion, which can only multiply suffering. Now it seems to me that the statement that the suffering of mankind is one is inseparable from the statement that the consciousness of mankind is one.

JK: Suffering is part of our consciousness.

DB: But one doesn't get the feeling immediately that this suffering belongs to the whole of mankind, you see.

JK: The world is me: I am the world. But we have divided it up into the British earth, and the French earth, and all the rest of it!

DB: Do you mean by the world, the physical world, or the world of society?

JK: The world of society, primarily the psychological world.

DB: So we say the world of society, of human beings, is one, and when I say I am that world, what does it mean?

JK: The world is not different from me.

DB: The world and I are one. We are inseparable.

JK: Yes. And that is real meditation; you must feel this, not just as a verbal statement: it is an actuality. I am my brother's keeper.

DB: Many religions have said that.

JK: That is just a verbal statement and they don't keep it; they don't do it in their hearts.

DB: Perhaps some have done it, but in general it is not being done?

JK: I don't know if anybody has done it. We human beings haven't done it. Our religions actually have prevented it.

DB: Because of division? Every religion has its own beliefs and its own organization.

JK: Of course. Its own gods and its own saviors.

DB: Yes.

JK: So from that, is that intelligence actual? You understand my question? Or is it some kind of fanciful projection, hoping that it will solve our problems? It is not to me. It is an actuality. Because the ending of suffering means love.

DB: Before we go on, let's clear up a point about "me." You see you said it is not to me. Now in some sense it seems that you are still defining an individual. Is that right?

JK: Yes. I am using the word "I" as a means of communication.

DB: But what does it mean? In some way, let's say there may be two people, let's say "A," who is the way you see, and "B" who is not, eh?

JK: Yes.

DB: So "A" says it is not—that seems to create a division between "A" and "B."

JK: That's right. But "B" creates the division.

DB: Why?

JK: What is the relationship between the two?

DB: "B" is creating the division by saying, "I am a separate person" but it may confuse "B" further when "A" says "It's not that way to me"—right?

JK: That is the whole point, isn't it, in relationship? You feel that you are not separate, and that you really have this sense of love and compassion, and I haven't got it. I haven't even perceived or gone into this question. What is your relationship to me? You have a relationship with me but I haven't any relationship with you.

DB: Well I think one could say that the person who hasn't seen is almost living a world of dreams, psychologically, and therefore the world of dreams is not related to the world of being awake.

JK: That's right.

DB: But the fellow who is awake can at least perhaps awaken the other fellow.

JK: You are awake; I am not. Then your relationship with me is very clear. But I have no relationship with you; I cannot have one. I insist on division, and you don't.

DB: Yes, we have to say that in some way the consciousness of mankind has divided itself, it is all one but it has divided itself by thought. And that is why we are in this situation.

JK: *That* is why. All the problems that humanity has now, psychologically, as well in other ways, are the result of thought. And we are pursuing the same pattern of thought, and thought will never solve any of these problems. So there is another kind of instrument, which is intelligence.

DB: Well that opens up an entirely different subject. And you mentioned love as well. And compassion.

JK: Without love and compassion there is no intelligence. And you cannot be compassionate if you are attached to some religion, if you are tied to a post like an animal. . . .

DB: Yes as soon as the self is threatened, then it cannot. . . .

JK: You see, self hides behind . . .

DB: . . . other things. I mean, noble ideals.

JK: Yes, it has immense capacity to hide itself. So what is the future of humanity? From what one observes it is leading to destruction.

DB: That is the way it seems to be going.

JK: Very gloomy, grim, and dangerous. If one has children, what is their future? To enter into all this? And go through the misery of it all. So education becomes extraordinarily important. But now education is merely the accumulation of knowledge.

DB: Every instrument that man has invented, discovered, or developed has been turned toward destruction.

JK: Absolutely. They are destroying nature; there are very few tigers now.

DB: They are destroying forests and agricultural land.

JK: Nobody seems to care.

DB: Well, most people are just immersed in their plans to save themselves, but others have plans to save humanity. I think also there is a tendency toward despair, implicit in what is happening now, in that people don't think anything can be done.

JK: Yes. And if they think something can be done they form little groups and little theories.

DB: There are those who are very confident in what they are doing. . . .

JK: Most prime ministers are very confident. They don't know what they are doing really!

DB: Yes but then most people haven't much confidence in what they are doing themselves.

JK: I know. And if someone has tremendous confidence I accept that confidence and go with them.

What is the future of mankind, the future of humanity? I wonder if anybody is concerned with it? Or whether each person, each group, is only concerned with its own survival?

DB: I think the first concern almost always has been with survival in either the individual or the group. That has been the history of mankind.

JK: Therefore, perpetual wars, perpetual insecurity.

DB: Yes, but this, as you said, is the result of thought, which makes the mistake on the basis of being incomplete of identifying the self with the group, and so on.

JK: You happen to listen to all this. You agree to all this, you see the truth of all this. Those in power will not even listen to you.

DB: No.

JK: They are creating more and more misery, the world is becoming more and more dangerous. What is the point of our seeing something to be true, and what effect has it?

DB: It seems to me that if we think in terms of the effects we are bringing in the very thing which is behind the trouble—time! Then the response would be to get in quickly and do something to change the course of events.

JK: And therefore form a society, foundation, organization, and all the rest of it.

DB: But you see our mistake is to feel that we must think about something, although that thought is incomplete. We don't really know what is going on, and people have made theories about it, but they don't know.

JK: If that is the wrong question, then as a human being, who is mankind, what is my responsibility, apart from effect, and all the rest of it?

DB: Yes, we can't look toward effects. But it is the same as with "A" and "B," that "A" sees, and "B" does not.

JK: Yes.

DB: Now suppose "A" sees something and most of the rest of mankind does not. Then, it seems, one could say mankind is in a sense dreaming, asleep.

JK: It is caught in illusion.

DB: Illusion. And the point is that, if somebody sees something, his responsibility is to help awaken the others out of the illusions.

JK: That is just it. This has been the problem. That is why the Buddhists have projected the idea of the Bodhisattva, who is the essence of all compassion, and is waiting to save humanity. It sounds nice. It is a happy feeling that there is somebody doing this. But in actuality we won't do anything that is not comfortable, satisfying, secure, both psychologically and physically.

DB: That is basically the source of the illusion.

JK: How does one make others see all this? They haven't time, they haven't the energy, they haven't even the inclination. They want to be amused. How does one make "X" see this whole thing so clearly that he says, "All right, I have got it, I will work. And I see I am responsible," and all the rest of it. I think that is the tragedy of those who see and those who don't.

Brockwood Park, England
11th June 1983

TWO

J. KRISHNAMURTI: Are all the psychologists, as far as we can understand, really concerned with the future of humanity? Or are they concerned with the human being conforming to the present society? Or going beyond that?

DAVID BOHM: I think that most psychologists evidently want the human being to conform to this society, but I think some are thinking of going beyond that, to transform the consciousness of mankind.

JK: Can the consciousness of mankind be changed through time? That is one of the questions we should discuss.

DB: Yes. We have discussed it already and I think what came out was that with regard to consciousness time is not relevant, that it is a kind of illusion. We discussed the illusion of becoming.

JK: We are saying, aren't we, that the evolution of consciousness is a fallacy.

DB: As through time, yes. Though physical evolution is not.

JK: Can we put it this way, much more simply? There is no psychological evolution, or evolution of the psyche?

DB: Yes. And, since the future of humanity depends on the psyche, it seems then that the future of humanity is not going to be determined through actions in time. And then that leaves us the question: what will we do?

JK: Now let's proceed from there. Shouldn't we first distinguish between the brain and the mind?

DB: Well that distinction has been made, and it is not clear. Now of course there are several views. One that the mind is just a function of the brain—that is the materialists' view. There is another view which says mind and brain are two different things.

JK: Yes, I think they are two different things.

DB: But there must be . . .

JK: . . . a contact between the two.

DB: Yes.

JK: A relationship between the two.

DB: We don't necessarily imply any separation of the two.

JK: No. First let's see the brain. I am really not an expert on the structure of the brain and all that kind of thing. But one can see within one, one can observe from one's own activity of the brain, that it is really like a computer which has been programmed, and remembers.

DB: Certainly a large part of the activity is that way, but one is not certain that all of it is that way.

JK: No. And it is conditioned.

DB: Yes.

JK: Conditioned by past generations, by the society, by the newspapers, by the magazines, by all the activities and pressures from the outside. It is conditioned.

DB: Now what do you mean by this conditioning?

JK: The brain is programmed; it is made to conform to a certain pattern; it lives entirely on the past, modifying itself with the present and going on.

DB: We have agreed that some of this conditioning is useful and necessary.

JK: Of course.

DB: But the conditioning which determines the self, you know, which determines the . . .

JK: . . . the psyche. Let's call it for the moment the psyche. The self.

DB: The self, the psyche, that conditioning is what you are talking about. That may not only be unnecessary but harmful.

JK: Yes. The emphasis on the psyche, on giving importance to the self, is creating great damage in the world, because it is separative and therefore it is constantly in conflict, not only within itself but with the society, with the family, and so on.

DB: Yes. And it is also in conflict with nature.

JK: With nature, with the whole universe.

DB: We have said that the conflict arose because . . .

JK: . . . of division. . . .

DB: The division arising because thought is limited. Being based on this conditioning, on knowledge and memory, it is limited.

JK: Yes. And experience is limited, therefore knowledge is limited; memory and thought. And the very structure and nature of the psyche is the movement of thought.

DB: Yes.

JK: In time.

DB: Yes. Now I would like to ask a question. You discussed the movement of thought but it doesn't seem clear to me what is moving. You see, if I discuss the movement of my hand, that is a real movement. It is clear what is meant. But now, when we discuss the movement of thought, it seems to me we are discussing something which is a kind of illusion, because you have said that becoming is the movement of thought.

JK: That is what I mean, the movement is becoming.

DB: But you are saying that movement is in some way illusory, aren't you?

JK: Yes, of course.

DB: It is rather like the movement on the screen which is projected from the camera. We say that there are no objects moving across the screen, but the only real movement is the turning of the projector. Now can we say that there is a real movement in the brain which is projecting all this, which is the conditioning?

JK: That is what we want to find out. Let's discuss that a bit. We both agree, or see, that the brain is conditioned.

DB: We mean that really it has been impressed physically, and chemically. . . .

JK: And genetically, as well as psychologically.

DB: What is the difference between physically and psychologically?

JK: Psychologically the brain is centred in the self—right?

DB: Yes.

JK: And the constant assertion of the self is the movement, the conditioning, an illusion.

DB: But there is some real movement happening inside. The brain, for example, is doing something. It has been conditioned physically and chemically. And something is happening physcially and chemically when we are thinking of the self.

JK: Are you asking whether the brain and the self are two different things?

DB: No, I am saying that the self is the result of conditioning the brain.

JK: Yes. The self is conditioning the brain.

DB: But does the self exist?

JK: No.

DB: But the conditioning of the brain, as I see it, is the involvement with an illusion which we call the self.

JK: That's right. Can that conditioning be dissipated? That's the whole question.

DB: It really has to be dissipated in some physical and chemical and neuro-physiological sense.

JK: Yes.

DB: Now the first reaction of any scientific person would be that it looks unlikely that we could dissipate it by the sort of thing we are doing. You see, some scientists might feel that maybe we will discover drugs or new genetic changes or deep knowledge of the structure of the brain. In that way we could perhaps help to do something. I think that idea might be current among some people.

JK: Will that change human behavior?

DB: Why not? I think some people believe it might.

JK: Wait a minute. That is the whole point. It *might,* which means in the future.

DB: Yes, it would take time to discover all this.

JK: In the meantime man is going to destroy himself.

DB: They might hope that he will manage to discover it in time. They could also criticize what we are doing, saying what good can it do? You see, it doesn't seem to affect anybody, and certainly not in time to make a big difference.

JK: We two are very clear about it. In what way does it affect humanity?

DB: Will it really affect mankind in time to save . . .

JK: Obviously not.

DB: Then why should we be doing it?

JK: Because this is the right thing to do. Independently. It has nothing to do with reward and punishment.

DB: Nor with goals. We do the right thing even though we don't know what the outcome will be?

JK: That's right.

DB: Are you saying there is no other way?

JK: We are saying there is no other way; that's right.

DB: Well we should make that clear. For example, some psychologists would feel that, by enquiring into this sort of thing, we could bring about an evolutionary transformation of consciousness.

JK: We come back to the point that through time we hope to change consciousness. We question that.

DB: We have questioned that, and are saying that through time, inevitably we are all caught in becoming and illusion, and we will not know what we are doing.

59

JK: That's right.

DB: Now could we say that the same thing would hold even for those scientists who are trying to do it physically and chemically or structurally; that they themselves are still caught in this, and through time they are caught in trying to become better?

JK: Yes. The experimentalists and the psychologists and ourselves are all trying to become something.

DB: Yes, though it may not seem obvious at first. It may seem that the scientists are really just disinterested, unbiased observers, working on the problem. But underneath one feels there is the desire to become better on the part of the person who is enquiring in that way.

JK: To become. Of course.

DB: He is not free of that.

JK: That is just it.

DB: And that desire will give rise to self-deception and illusion, and so on.

JK: So where are we now? Any form of becoming is an illusion, and becoming implies time, time for the psyche to change. But we are saying that time is not necessary.

DB: Now that ties up with the other question of the mind and the brain. The brain is an activity in time, as a physical, chemical, complex process.

JK: I think the mind is separate from the brain.

DB: What does separate mean? Are they in contact?

JK: Separate in the sense that the brain is conditioned and the mind is not.

DB: Let's say the mind has a certain independence of the brain. Even if the brain is conditioned . . .

JK: . . . the other is not.

DB: It need not be . . .

JK: . . . conditioned.

DB: On what basis do you say that?

JK: Let's not begin on what basis I say that.

DB: Well, what makes you say it?

JK: As long as the brain is conditioned, it is not free.

DB: Yes.

JK: And the mind *is* free.

DB: Yes, that is what you are saying. But you see, the brain not being free means that it is not free to enquire in an unbiased way.

JK: I will go into it. Let's enquire what is freedom? Freedom to enquire, freedom to investigate. It is only in freedom that there is deep insight.

DB: Yes, that's clear, because if you are not free to enquire, or if you are biased, then you are limited, in an arbitrary way.

JK: So as long as the brain is conditioned its relationship to the mind is limited.

DB: We have the relationship of the brain to the mind, and also the other way round.

JK: Yes. But the mind being free has a relationship to the brain.

DB: Yes. Now we say the mind is free, in some sense, not subject to the conditioning of the brain.

JK: Yes.

DB: What is the nature of the mind? Is the mind located inside the body, or is it in the brain?

JK: No, it is nothing to do with the body or the brain.

DB: Has it to do with space or time?

JK: Space—now wait a minute! It has to do with space and silence. These are the two factors of the . . .

DB: But not time?

JK: Not time. Time belongs to the brain.

DB: You say space and silence; now what kind of space? It is not the space in which we see life moving.

JK: Space. Let's look round at it the other way. Thought can invent space.

DB: In addition, we have the space that we see. But thought can invent all kinds of space.

JK: And space from here to there.

DB: Yes, the space through which we move is that way.

JK: Space also between two noises, two sounds.

DB: They call that the interval, the interval between two sounds.

JK: Yes, the interval between two noises. Two thoughts. Two notes.

DB: Yes.

JK: Space between two people.

DB: Space between the walls.

JK: And so on. But that kind of space is not the space of the mind.

DB: You say it is not limited?

JK: That's right. But I didn't want to use the word limited.

DB: But it is implied. That kind of space is not in the nature of being bounded by something.

JK: No, it is not bounded by the psyche.

DB: But is it bounded by anything?

JK: No. So can the brain, with all its cells conditioned, can those cells radically change?

DB: We have often discussed this. It is not certain that all the cells are conditioned. For example, some people think that only some or a small part of the cells are being used, and that the others are just inactive, dormant.

JK: Hardly used at all, or just touched occasionally.

DB: Just touched occasionally. But those cells that are conditioned, whatever they may be, evidently dominate consciousness now.

JK: Yes. Can those cells be changed?

DB: Yes.

JK: We are saying that they can, through insight; insight being out of time, not the result of remembrance, not an intuition, nor desire, nor hope. It is nothing to do with any time and thought.

DB: Yes. Now is insight of the mind? Is it of the nature of mind? An activity of mind?

JK: Yes.

DB: Therefore you are saying that mind can act in the matter of the brain.

JK: Yes, we said that earlier.

DB: But, you see, this point, how mind is able to act in matter, is difficult.

JK: It is able to act on the brain. For instance, take any crisis, or problem. The root meaning of problem is, as you know, "something thrown at you." And we meet it with all the remembrance of the past, with a bias and so on. And therefore the problem multiplies itself. You may solve one problem, but in the very solution of one particular problem, other problems arise, as happens in politics, and so on. Now to approach the problem, or to have perception of it without any past memories and thoughts interfering or projecting . . .

DB: That implies that perception also is of the mind. . . .

JK: Yes, that's right.

DB: Are you saying that the brain is a kind of instrument of the mind?

JK: An instrument of the mind when the brain is not self-centered.

DB: All the conditioning may be thought of as the brain exciting itself, and keeping itself going just from the program. This occupies all of its capacities.

JK: All our days, yes.

DB: The brain is rather like a radio receiver which can generate its own noise, but would not pick up a signal.

JK: Not quite. Let's go into this a little. Experience is always limited. I may blow up that experience into something fantastic, and then set up a shop to sell my experience, but that experience is limited. And so knowledge is always limited. And this knowledge is operating in the brain. This knowledge is the brain. And thought is also part of the brain, and thought is limited. So the brain is operating in a very, very small area.

DB: Yes. What prevents it from operating in a broader area? In an unlimited area?

JK: Thought.

DB: But it seems to me the brain is running on its own, from its own program.

65

JK: Yes, like a computer.

DB: Essentially, what you are asking is that the brain should really be responding to the mind.

JK: It can only respond if it is free from the limited; from thought, which is limited.

DB: So the program does not then dominate it. You see we are still going to need that program.

JK: Of course. We need it for . . .

DB: . . . for many things. But is intelligence from the mind?

JK: Yes, intelligence is the mind.

DB: Is the mind.

JK: We must go into something else. Because compassion is related to intelligence, there is no intelligence without compassion. And compassion can only be, when there is love which is completely free from all remembrances, personal jealousies, and so on.

DB: Is all that compassion, love, also of the mind?

JK: Of the mind. You cannot be compassionate if you are attached to any particular experience, or any particular ideal.

DB: Yes, that is again the program.

JK: Yes. For instance, there are those people who go out to various poverty-ridden countries and work, work, work. And they call that compassion. But they are attached, or tied to a particular form of religious belief, and therefore their action is merely pity or sympathy. It is not compassion.

DB: Yes, I understand that we have here two things which can be somewhat independent. There is the brain and the mind, though they make contact. Then we say that intelligence and compassion come from beyond the brain. Now I would like to go into the question of how they are making contact.

JK: Ah! Contact can only exist between the mind and the brain when the brain is quiet.

DB: Yes, that is the requirement for making it. The brain has got be be quiet.

JK: Quiet is not a trained quietness. Not a self-conscious, meditative, desire for silence. It is a natural outcome of understanding one's own conditioning.

DB: And one can see that if the brain is quiet it could listen to something deeper?

JK: That's right. Then if it is quiet it is related to the mind. Then the mind can function through the brain.

DB: I think that it would help if we could see with regard to the brain whether it has any activity which is beyond thought. You see, for example, one could ask, is awareness part of the function of the brain?

JK: As long as it is awareness in which there is no choice.

DB: I think that may cause difficulty. What is wrong with choice?

JK: Choice means confusion.

DB: That is not obvious. . . .

JK: After all, you have to choose between two things.

DB: I could choose whether I will buy one thing or another.

JK: Yes, I can choose between this table and that table.

DB: I choose the colors when I buy the table. That need not be confused. If I choose which color I want, I don't see why that has to be confused.

JK: There is nothing wrong. There is no confusion there.

DB: But it seems to me that the choice about the psyche is where the confusion is.

JK: That's all; we are talking of the psyche that chooses.

DB: That chooses to become.

JK: Yes. Chooses to become. And choice exists where there is confusion.

DB: Are you saying that out of confusion the psyche makes a choice to become one thing or another? Being confused, it tries to become something better?

JK: And choice implies a duality.

DB: But it seems at first sight that we have another duality which you have introduced, which is the mind and the brain.

JK: No, that is not a duality.

DB: What is the difference?

JK: Let's take a very simple example. Human beings are violent, and nonviolence has been projected by thought. That is the duality—the the fact, and the non-fact.

DB: You are saying there is a duality between a fact, and some mere projection which the mind makes.

JK: The ideal and the fact.

DB: The ideal is non-real, and the fact is real.

JK: That's it. The ideal is not actual.

DB: Yes. Now then you say the division of those is duality. Why do you give it that name?

JK: Because they are divided.

DB: Well at least they appear to be divided.

JK: Divided, and we are struggling. For instance, all the totalitarian communist ideals, and the democratic ideals, are the outcome of thought which is limited, and this is creating havoc in the world.

DB: So there is a division which has been brought in. But I think we were discussing in terms of dividing something which cannot be divided. Of trying to divide the psyche.

JK: That's right. Violence cannot be divided into non-violence.

DB: And the psyche cannot be divided into violence and nonviolence. Right?

JK: It is what it is.

DB: It is what it is; so, if it is violent, it can't be divided into a violent and a nonviolent part.

JK: So can we remain with "what is," not with "what should be," "what must be," not invent ideals, and so on?

DB: Yes, but could we return to the question of the mind and the brain? Now we are saying that is not a division.

JK: Oh no, that is not a division.

DB: They are in contact, is that right?

JK: We said, there is contact between the mind and the brain when the brain is silent and has space.

DB: So we are saying that although they are in contact and not divided at all, the mind can still have a certain independence of the conditioning of the brain.

JK: Now let's be careful! Suppose my brain is conditioned, for example, programmed as a Hindu, and my whole life and action are conditioned by the idea that I am a Hindu. Mind obviously has no relationship with that conditioning.

DB: You are using the word mind; not *"my"* mind.

JK: Mind. It is not "mine."

DB: It is universal or general.

JK: Yes. And it is not "my" brain either.

DB: No, but there is a particular brain, this brain or that brain. Would you say that there is a particular mind?

JK: No.

DB: That is an important difference. You are saying mind is really universal.

JK: Mind is universal—if you can use that ugly word.

DB: Unlimited and undivided.

JK: It is unpolluted; not polluted by thought.

DB: But I think for most people there will be difficulty in saying how we know anything about this mind. We only know that my mind is the first feeling—right?

JK: You cannot call it *your* mind. You only have *your* brain, which is conditioned. You can't say, "It is *my* mind."

DB: But whatever is going on inside I feel is mine, and it is very different from what is going on inside somebody else.

JK: No, I question whether it is different.

71

DB: At least it seems different.

JK: Yes. I question whether it *is* different, what is going on inside me as a human being, and you as another human being. We both go through all kinds of problems: suffering, fear, anxiety, loneliness, and so on. We have our dogmas, beliefs, superstitions. And everybody has this.

DB: We can say it is all very similar, but it seems as if each one of us is isolated from the other.

JK: By thought. My thought has created the belief that I am different from you, because my body is different from yours, my face is different from yours. We extend that same thing into the psychological area.

DB: But now if we said that division is an illusion, perhaps?

JK: No, not perhaps! It *is.*

DB: It is an illusion. All right. Although it is not obvious when a person first looks at it.

JK: Of course.

DB: In reality even brain is not divided, because we are saying that we are all not only basically similar but really connected. And then we say beyond all that is mind, which has no division at all.

JK: It is unconditioned.

DB: Yes, it would almost seem to imply, then, that in so far as a person feels he is a separate being he has very little contact with mind.

JK: Quite right. That is what we said.

DB: No mind.

JK: That is why it is very important to understand not the mind but our conditioning. And whether our conditioning, human conditioning, can ever be dissolved. That is the real issue.

DB: Yes. I think we still want to understand the meaning of what is being said. You see, we have a mind that is universal; that is in some kind of space, you say, or is it its own space?

JK: It is not in me or in my brain.

DB: But it has a space.

JK: It is, it lives in space and silence.

DB: It lives in a space and silence, but it is the space of the mind. It is not a space like this space?

JK: No. That is why we said space is not invented by thought.

DB: Yes, now is it possible then to perceive this space when the mind is silent, to be in contact with it?

JK: Not perceive. Let's see. You are asking whether the mind can be perceived by the brain.

DB: Or at least the brain somehow be aware . . . an awareness, a sense.

JK: We are saying, yes; through meditation. You may not like to use that word.

73

DB: I don't mind.

JK: You see, the difficulty is that when you use the word "meditation" it is generally understood that there is always a meditator meditating. Real meditation is an unconscious process, not a conscious process.

DB: How then are you able to say that meditation takes place if it is unconscious?

JK: It is taking place when the brain is quiet.

DB: You mean by consciousness all the movement of thought? Feeling, desire, will, and all that goes with it?

JK: Yes.

DB: There is a kind of awareness still, isn't there?

JK: Oh yes. It depends what you call awareness. Awareness of what?

DB: Possibly awareness of something deeper, I don't know.

JK: Again, when you use the word "deeper," it is a measurement. I wouldn't use that.

DB: Well, let's not use that. But, you see, there is a kind of unconsciousness which we are simply not aware of at all. A person may be unconscious of some of his problems, conflicts.

JK: Let's go at it a bit more. If I do something consciously, it is the activity of thought.

DB: Yes, it is thought reflecting on itself.

74

JK: Right, it is the activity of thought. Now if I consciously meditate, practise, do all that, which I call nonsense, then I am making the brain conform to another series of patterns.

DB: Yes, it is more becoming.

JK: More becoming, that's right.

DB: You are trying to become better.

JK: There is no illumination by becoming. One can't be illumed, if I can use that word, by saying that one is going to be some sort of guru.

DB: But it seems very difficult to communicate something which is not conscious.

JK: That's it. That's the difficulty.

DB: It is not just being knocked out. If a person is unconscious, he is knocked out, but you don't mean that.

JK: Of course not!

DB: Or under anesthetic or . . .

JK: No, let's put it this way: conscious meditation, conscious activity to control thought, to free oneself from conditioning, is not freedom.

DB: Yes, I think that is clear, but it becomes very unclear how to communicate something else.

JK: Wait a minute. You want to discuss what lies beyond thought.

DB: Or when thought is silent.

JK: Quiet, silent. What words would you use?

DB: Well, I suggested the word awareness. What about the word attention?

JK: Attention for me is better. Would you say, in attention there is no center as the me?

DB: Well, not in the kind of attention you are discussing. There is the usual kind, where we pay attention because of what interests us.

JK: Attention is not concentration.

DB: We are discussing a kind of attention without this "me" present, which is not the activity of the conditioning.

JK: Not the activity of thought. In attention, thought has no place.

DB: Yes, but could we say more? What do you mean by attention? Now would the derivation of the word be of any use? It means stretching the mind—would that help?

JK: No. Would it help if we say concentration is not attention? Effort is not attention. When I make an effort to attend it is not attention. Attention can only come into being when the self is not.

DB: Yes, but that is going to get us in a circle, because usually we are starting when the self is.

JK: No, I used the word carefully. Meditation means measure.

DB: Yes.

JK: As long as there is measurement, which is becoming, there is no meditation. Let's put it that way.

DB: Yes. We can discuss when there is not meditation.

JK: That's right. Through negation the other is.

DB: Because if we succeed in negating the whole activity of what is not meditation, the meditation will be there.

JK: That's right.

DB: That which is not meditation, but which we think is meditation.

JK: Yes, that is very clear. As long as there is measurement, which is the becoming, which is the process of thought, meditation or silence cannot be.

DB: Is this undirected attention mind?

JK: Attention is of the mind.

DB: Well, it contacts the brain, doesn't it?

JK: Yes. As long as the brain is silent, the other has contact.

DB: That is, this true attention has contact with the brain, when the brain is silent.

JK: Silent, and has space.

DB: What is the space?

JK: The brain has no space now, because it is concerned with itself, it is programmed, it is self-centered and it is limited.

DB: Yes. The mind is in its space; now does the brain have its space too? Limited space?

JK: Of course. Thought has a limited space.

DB: But when thought is absent, does the brain have its space?

JK: Yes. The brain has space.

DB: Unlimited?

JK: No. It is only mind that has unlimited space.
   My brain can be quiet over a problem which I have thought about, and I suddenly say, "Well I won't think anymore about it," and there is a certain amount of space. In that space you solve the problem.

DB: Now if the brain is silent, if it is not thinking of a problem, then still the space is limited, but it is open to . . .

JK: . . . to the other.

DB: . . . to the attention. Would you say that, through attention, or in attention, the mind is contacting the brain?

JK: When the brain is not inattentive.

DB: So what happens to the brain?

JK: What happens to the brain which is to act? Let's get it clear. We said intelligence is born out of compassion and love. That intelligence operates when the brain is quiet.

DB: Yes. Does it operate through attention?

JK: Of course.

DB: So attention seems to be the contact.

JK: Naturally. We said too that attention can only be, when the self is not.

DB: Now you say that love and compassion are the ground, and out of this comes the intelligence, through attention.

JK: Yes, it functions through the brain.

DB: So there are two questions: one is the nature of this intelligence, and the second is, what does it do to the brain?

JK: Yes, let's see. We must again approach it negatively. Love is not jealousy, and all that. Love is not personal, but it can be personal.

DB: Then it is not what you are talking about.

JK: Love is not *my* country, *your* country, or "I love *my* god." It is not that.

DB: If it is from universal mind. . . .

JK: That is why I say love has no relationship to thought.

DB: And it does not start in the particular brain, does not originate in the particular brain.

JK: When there is that love, out of it there is compassion and there is intelligence.

DB: Is this intelligence able to understand deeply?

JK: No, not "understand."

DB: What does it do? Does it perceive?

JK: Through perception it acts.

DB: Perception of what?

JK: Now let's discuss perception. There can be perception only when it is not tinged by thought. When there is no interference from the movement of thought, there is perception, which is direct insight into a problem, or into human complexities.

DB: Now this perception originates in the mind?

JK: Does the perception originate in the mind? Yes. When the brain is quiet.

DB: But we use the words perception and intelligence, now how are they related, or what is their difference?

JK: The difference between perception and intelligence?

DB: Yes.

JK: None.

DB: So we can say intelligence is perception.

JK: Yes, that's right.

DB: Intelligence is perception of "what is"? And through attention there is contact.

JK: Let's take a problem, then it is easier to understand. Take the problem of suffering. Human beings have suffered endlessly, through wars, through physical disease, and through wrong relationship with each other. Now can that end?

DB: I would say the difficulty of ending that is that it is on the program. We are conditioned to this whole thing.

JK: Yes. Now that has been going on for centuries.

DB: So it is very deep.

JK: Very, very deep. Now can that suffering end?

DB: It cannot end by an action of the brain.

JK: By thought.

DB: Because the brain is caught in suffering, and it cannot take an action to end its own suffering.

JK: Of course it cannot. That is why thought cannot end it. Thought has created it.

DB: Yes, thought has created it, and anyway it is unable to get hold of it.

81

JK: Thought has created the wars, the misery, the confusion. And thought has become prominent in human relationship.

DB: Yes, but I think people might agree with that and still think that just as thought can do bad things, it can do good things.

JK: No, thought cannot do good or bad. It is thought, limited.

DB: Thought cannot get hold of this suffering. That is, this suffering being in the physical and chemical conditioning of the brain, thought has no way of even knowing what it is.

JK: I mean, I lose my son and I am. . . .

DB: Yes, but by thinking, I don't know what is going on inside me. I can't change the suffering inside because thinking will not show me what it is. Now you are saying intelligence is perception.

JK: But we are asking, can suffering end? That is the problem.

DB: Yes, and it is clear that thinking cannot end it.

JK: Thought cannot do it. That is the point. If I have an insight into it . . .

DB: Now this insight will be through the action of the mind; through intelligence and attention.

JK: When there is that insight, intelligence wipes away suffering.

82

DB: You are saying, therefore, that there is a contact from mind to matter which removes the whole physical, chemical structure that keeps us going on with suffering.

JK: That's right. In that ending there is a mutation in the brain cells.

DB: Yes, and that mutation just wipes out the whole structure that makes you suffer.

JK: That's right. Therefore it is as if I have been going along a certain tradition; I suddenly change that tradition and there is a change in the whole brain, which has been going North. Now it goes East.

DB: Of course this is a radical notion from the point of view of traditional ideas in science, because, if we accept that mind is different from matter, then people would find it hard to say that mind would actually . . .

JK: Would you put it that mind is pure energy?

DB: Well, we could put it that way, but matter is energy too.

JK: But matter is limited; thought is limited.

DB: But we are saying that the pure energy of mind is able to reach into the limited energy of matter?

JK: Yes, that's right. And change the limitation.

DB: Remove some of the limitation.

JK: When there is a deep issue, problem, or challenge which you are facing.

DB: We could also add that all the traditional ways of trying to do this cannot work. . . .

JK: They haven't worked.

DB: Well, that is not enough. We have to say, because people still might hope it could, that it cannot, actually.

JK: It cannot.

DB: Because thought cannot get at its own physical, chemical basis in the cells, and do anything about those cells.

JK: Yes. Thought cannot bring about a change in itself.

DB: And yet practically everything that mankind has been trying to do is based on thought. There is a limited area, of course, where that is all right, but we cannot do anything about the future of humanity from that usual approach.

JK: When one listens to the politicians, who are so very active in the world, they are creating problem after problem, and to them thought, ideals are the most important things.

DB: Generally speaking nobody knows of anything else.

JK: Exactly. We are saying that the old instrument which is thought is worn out, except in certain areas.

DB: It never was adequate, except in those areas.

JK: Of course.

DB: And, as far as history goes, man has always been in trouble.

JK: Man has always been in trouble, in turmoil, in fear. And facing all the confusion of the world, can there be a solution to all this?

DB: That comes back to the question I would like to repeat. It seems there are a few people who are talking about it, and think perhaps they know, or perhaps they meditate, and so on. But how is that going to affect this vast current of mankind?

JK: Probably very little. But why will it affect this? It might, or it might not. But then one puts that question: what is the use of it?

DB: Yes, that's the point. I think there is an instinctive feeling that makes one put the question.

JK: But I think that is the wrong question.

DB: You see, the first instinct is to say, "What can we do to stop this tremendous catastrophe?"

JK: Yes. But if each one of us, whoever listens, sees the truth that thought, in its activity both externally and inwardly, has created a terrible mess, great suffering, then one must inevitably ask is there an ending to all this? If thought cannot end it, what will?

DB: Yes.

JK: What is the new instrument that will put an end to all this misery? You see, there is a new instrument which is the mind, which is intelligence. But the difficulty is also that people won't listen to all this. Both the scientists and the ordinary laymen like us, have come to definite conclusions, and they won't listen.

DB: Yes, well, that is what I had in mind when I said that a few people don't seem to have much effect.

JK: Of course. I think, after all, few people have changed the world, whether good or bad—but that is not the point. Hitler; and also the communists have changed it, but they have gone to the same pattern again. Physical revolution has never psychologically changed the human state.

DB: Do you think it is possible that a certain number of brains coming in contact with mind in this way will be able to have an effect on mankind, which is beyond just the immediate, obvious effect of their communication?

JK: Yes, that's right. But how do you convey this subtle and very complex issue to a person who is steeped in tradition, who is conditioned, and won't even take time to listen, to consider?

DB: Well, that is the question. You see, you could say that this conditioning cannot be absolute; cannot be an absolute block, or else there would be no way out at all. But the conditioning may be thought to have some sort of permeability.

JK: I mean, after all, the pope won't listen to us, but the pope has tremendous influence.

DB: Is it possible that every person has something he can listen to, if it could be found?

JK: If he has a little patience. Who will listen? The politicians won't listen. The idealists won't listen. The totalitarians won't listen. The deeply steeped religious people won't listen. So perhaps a so-called ignorant person, not highly educated or conditioned in his professional career, or by money, the poor man who says, "I am suffering, please let's end that." . . .

DB: But he doesn't listen either, you see. He wants to get a job.

JK: Of course. He says, "Feed me first." We have been through all this for the last sixty years. The poor man won't listen, the rich man won't listen, the learned won't listen, and the deeply dogmatic religious believers don't listen. So perhaps it is like a wave in the world; it might catch somebody. I think it is a wrong question to say, does it affect?

DB: Yes, all right. We will say that that brings in time, and that is becoming. It brings in the psyche in the process of becoming again.

JK: Yes. But if you say . . . it must affect mankind . . .

DB: Are you proposing that it affects mankind through the mind directly, rather than through . . .

JK: Yes. It may not show immediately in action.

DB: You said that the mind is universal, and is not located in our ordinary space, is not separate. . . .

JK: Yes, but there is a danger in saying this, that the mind is universal. That is what some people say of the mind, and it has become a tradition.

DB: One can turn it into an idea, of course.

JK: That is just the danger of it; that is what I am saying.

DB: Yes. But really the question is, we have to come directly in contact with this to make it real. Right?

JK: That's it. We can only come into contact with it when the self is not. To put it very simply, when the self is not, there is beauty, silence, space; then that intelligence, which is born of compassion, operates through the brain. It is very simple.

DB: Yes. Would it be worth discussing the self, since the self is widely active?

JK: I know. That is our long tradition of many, many centuries.

DB: Is there some aspect of meditation which can be helpful here when the self is acting? You see, suppose a person says, "all right, I am caught in the self, but I want to get out. But I want to know what I shall do?"

JK: No.

DB: I won't use the words "what shall I do?" But what do you say?

JK: That is very simple. Is the observer different from the observed?

DB: Well, suppose we say, "Yes, it appears to be different"; then what?

JK: Is that an idea or an actuality?

DB: What do you mean?

JK: Actuality is when there is no division between the thinker and the thought.

DB: But suppose I say, ordinarily one feels that the observer is different from the observed. We begin there.

JK: We begin there. I'll show you. Look at it. Are you different from your anger, from your envy, from your suffering? You are not.

DB: At first sight it appears that I am, that I might try to control it.

JK: You are that.

DB: Yes, but how will I see that I am that?

JK: You are your name. You are your form, your body. You are the reactions and actions. You are the belief, the fear, the suffering and pleasure. You are all that.

DB: But the first experience is that I am here first, and that those are properties of me; they are my qualities which I can either have or not have. I might be angry, or not angry, I might have this belief, or that belief.

JK: Contradictory. You are all that.

DB: But you see, it is not obvious. When you say I am that, do you mean that I am that, and cannot be otherwise?

JK: No. At present you are that. It can be totally otherwise.

DB: All right. So I am all that. You are telling me that this unbiased observer is the same as the anger he is looking at?

JK: Of course. Just as I analyze myself, and the analyzer is the analyzed.

DB: Yes. He is biased by what he analyzes.

JK: Yes.

DB: So, if I watch anger for a while, I can see that I am very biased by the anger, so at some stage I say that I am one with that anger?

JK: No, not "I am one with it"; I am it.

DB: That anger and I are the same?

JK: Yes. The observer is the observed. And when that actuality exists you have really eliminated altogether conflict. Conflict exists when I am separate from my quality.

DB: Yes, that is because if I believe myself to be separate, then I can try to change it, but since I *am* that, it

90

is trying to change itself and remain itself at the same time.

JK: Yes, that's right. But when the quality is me, the division has ended. Right?

DB: When I see that the quality is me, then there is no point in trying to change.

JK: No. When there is division and the quality is not me, in that there is conflict, either suppression or escape, and so on, which is a wastage of energy. When that quality *is* me, all that energy which has been wasted is there to look, to observe.

DB: But why does it make such a difference to have that quality being me?

JK: It makes a difference when there is no division between the quality and me.

DB: Well then there is no perception of a difference....

JK: That's right. Put it round differently.

DB: . . . the mind does not try to fight itself.

JK: Yes, yes. It is so.

DB: If there is an illusion of a difference, the mind must be compelled to fight against itself.

JK: The brain.

DB: The brain fights against itself.

JK: That's right.

DB: On the other hand, when there is no illusion of a difference, the brain just stops fighting.

JK: And therefore you have tremendous energy.

DB: The brain's natural energy is released?

JK: Yes. And energy means attention.

DB: The energy of the brain allows for attention. . . .

JK: For that thing to dissolve.

DB: Yes, but wait a minute. We said before that attention was a contact of the mind and the brain.

JK: Yes.

DB: The brain must be in a state of high energy to allow that contact.

JK: That's right.

DB: I mean, a brain which is low energy cannot allow that contact.

JK: Of course not. But most of us are low energy because we are so conditioned.

DB: Well essentially you are saying that this is the way to start.

JK: Yes, start simply. Start with "what is," what I am. Self-knowledge is so important. It is not an accumulated process of knowledge, which one then looks at; it is a constant learning about oneself.

DB: If you call it self-knowledge, then it is not knowledge of the kind we talked about before, which is conditioning.

JK: That's right. Knowledge conditions.

DB: But you are saying that self-knowledge of this kind is not conditioning. But why do you call it knowledge? Is it a different kind of knowledge?

JK: Yes. Knowledge conditions.

DB: Yes, but now you have this self-knowledge.

JK: Which is to know and to comprehend oneself. To understand oneself is such a subtle, complex thing. It is living.

DB: Essentially knowing yourself in the very moment in which things are happening.

JK: Yes, to know what is happening.

DB: Rather than store it up in memory.

JK: Of course. Through reactions, I begin to discover what I am.

Brockwood Park, England
20th June 1983

Classic Works
from the Great Spiritual Teacher,
J. Krishnamurti

THE NETWORK OF THOUGHT

Krishnamurti here likens the condition of the human mind to the programming of a computer and offers his many readers an opportunity to form an independent network of thought. He describes the effect of inhibiting programs—received from family, society, environment, and education—in the growth of genuine awareness and offers an alternative to the particular "program" impressed on our individuality. Krishnamurti shows how to move beyond the illusion, fear, and conflict generated by programmed thinking, how to free ourselves from debilitating concepts of "I," and how to open ourselves to a "truth that is timeless, sacred, incorruptible."

THE FIRST AND LAST FREEDOM

Cutting away symbols and false associations, Krishnamurti continues the search for pure truth and perfect freedom. The freedom of which he writes is the breaking of the debilitating, consuming concern with the self. Once people find this first freedom, they are liberated from the unfulfilling and destructive obsessions of society. In *The First and Last Freedom,* the discussion ranges widely—on suffering, on fear, on gossip, on sex, among other topics—but continually returns to the core concept of freedom. Here Krishnamurti's quest becomes the reader's, an undertaking of tremendous significance.

KRISHNAMURTI'S JOURNAL

A uniquely personal spiritual document in which Krishnamurti records crucial periods of his own reflection. Mary Lutyens has sensitively edited this journal, which gives a rare glimpse into the mind of this world-renowned teacher. Krishnamurti blends past and present, reaching the furthest limits of his own consciousness. His words have the beauty and transparency of a prose-poem and provide the reader with a deeper knowledge of the self, the nature and function of meditation, and the true consciousness.

KRISHNAMURTI'S NOTEBOOK

"The best picture we have today of the life of the spirit outside a strictly religious context."—*Library Journal*

"Krishnamurti kept this luminous diary over a seven-month period. . . . At the book's core are ecstatic states of mind. . . . In the light of these he writes of the awareness that can only come when the brain is 'empty,' of radical aloneness, of the destruction of the known (experience, knowledge, conflict,time) so that the unknown may flower, of a love that lies beyond feeling and thought, of meditation that is not a system but an 'explosion.' Entwined with these are descriptions of the natural scene. . . . which, similar yet subtly different, testify to his claim that awareness is always new."—*Publishers Weekly*

FREEDOM FROM THE KNOWN

Krishnamurti shows here how people can free themselves radically and immediately form the tyranny of the expected, no matter what their age. And, by first changing themselves, people can then change the whole structure of society and their relationships. The vital need for change and the recognition of its very possibility constitute the rich essence of Krishnamurti's message in this classic work.

THE ENDING OF TIME J. KRISHNAMURTI AND DAVID BOHM

Penetrating dialouges between the great spiritual leader and the renowned physicist shed light on fundamental questions of existence. They discern the roots of psychological conflict in internalized conceptions of time which put us at odds with the true gound of being and deny the mind true insight. They discuss the importance of "cleansing the mind of the accumulation of time" and "breaking the pattern of ego-centered activity." New insights emerge on human thought, death, awakening insight, cosmic order, and the problem of the fragmented mind.

THE FLAME OF ATTENTION

In this selection of talks from a series given in India, England, Switzerland, and the United States in 1981 and 1982, Krishnamurti brings insight and compassion to bear on the problems of psychological insecurity and anxiety, and the solutions one finds through "attentiveness"—the key to true intelligence. By rejecting strict cause-and-effect thinking and religious, political, and philosophical conditioning, he shows we can give full attention to the world as it truly is, and find freedom form obsessive self-evaluation and its related psychological fears, anxieties, insecurity, hatred, sorrow, and violence.

Available from your local bookstore, or call 800–638–3030. We accept MasterCard, VISA, and personal checks.